contrasting elements

JAE MARIES

2

Contents

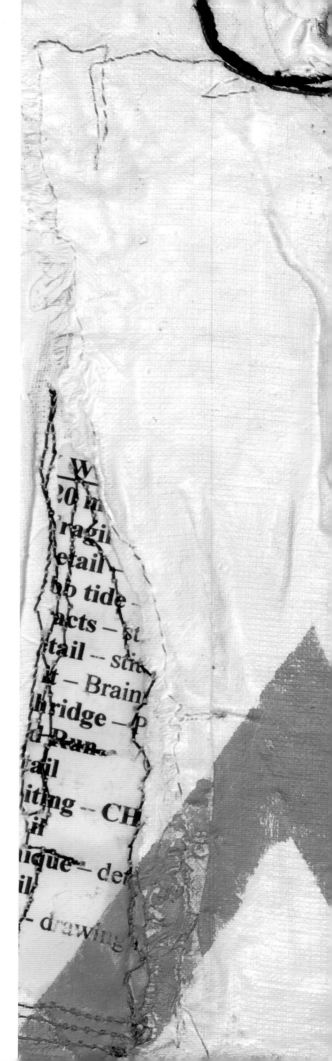

INTRODUCTION   4

CHAPTER 1 COLOUR CONTRASTS   8
ENERGY AND TRANQUILLITY   10
COLD AND WARM   14
MOOD SWINGS   19

CHAPTER 2 DYNAMIC DESIGN   22
CONFLICTING SCALE   24
EBB AND FLOW   28
FRICTION IN FORM   32

CHAPTER 3 MATERIAL BRAVURA   36
SHEEN AND MATT   38
STATIC AND FLUID   43
NATURAL AND SYNTHETIC   48

CHAPTER 4 OPPOSING PROCESSES   52
KNOTTING AND KNITTING   54
WEAVING AND WRAPPING   58
MANIPULATED FABRIC AND STITCH   62

CHAPTER 5 CHALLENGING IMAGERY   66
WORD PLAY   68
CREATING A MEMORY BOX   72
SKETCHBOOKS   74

RESOURCES   80

'Timelines' (detail).

This piece was constructed from unbleached calico (muslin), oil paint, printed fabrics, paper and hand and machine threads. The stitched calico base fabric was overlaid with oil paint. Fabric scraps, painting and hand and machine stitching were then added.

Introduction

Everyday life is full of many contrasts!

All contrasts can enliven your day, presenting both welcome and difficult challenges. As sources of inspiration, they can bring dynamism into your creative textile art work, making it more personally expressive, profound and individualistic.

The exciting contrasts highlighted in this book come under the following headings:

Colour – perhaps the first thing that comes to mind

Design – lots of ideas in this section

Materials – where unusual combinations form the dynamic

Techniques and imagery – offer a variety of contrast.

These new approaches will enable your art work to become refreshed and energised. You will be encouraged to explore your own personal ideas and resources with the aim of producing work that is unique and has its own original voice, something that we all strive for.

By working through the book, you will gain the extra confidence to continue to experiment, broaden your horizons and use your life experiences as the basis of new creative art textiles. Make it your life work! It's a small step away.

Detail from the piece on page 17.

'If there is light then there is darkness; if cold then heat; if height, depth also; if solid, then fluid; hardness and softness, roughness and smoothness, calm and tempest, prosperity and adversity, life and death.'

Pythagoras

HOW THE BOOK WORKS

The book encourages readers to work through a series of Skill Development exercises in both paper and fabric, usually with stitch. Step-by-step instructions describe a technique clearly and encourage further experiments. The materials required for each Skill Development will be listed at the beginning of every section. A list of suppliers is given at the back of the book and on the website www.d4daisy.com

WHO IS THIS BOOK FOR AND DO I NEED TO HAVE ANY EXPERIENCE?

The aim of this book is to motivate students who want to move their work forward and give it a distinctive individual quality.

Anyone and everyone who wants a challenge will relish this book and benefit from the experience of working through the activities.

People new to innovative textiles will enjoy exploring the fresh ideas and basic art concepts within and will gain a deeper understanding of design and colour for future work.

The more experienced embroiderer and textile artist will gather ideas to move their work forward. Through practice and a deeper thought process, you will gain the confidence to make sound aesthetic judgements to create distinctive personal art work.

Teachers will also gain from the book, discovering new ideas and approaches to enhance and energise their students' work.

A deeper expressiveness in any art work comes through experimentation and experience and this is accomplished by practising with the basic tools for the job. These will be outlined in each chapter. Use them, practise with them and the resulting work will become more personally expressive.

The techniques explored are very simple. There will be opportunities to expand them, to use your own experience and ways of working, as you make your way through the chapters.

This is part of the challenge. You are in control and you will use your judgement as to whether the piece is 'working' or not. The more you practise making these judgements, the less daunting those decisions will become in the future.

WORKING THROUGH THE BOOK

Why not begin with the chapter that has the most appeal to you or that offers you a captivating challenge? Then move on to other chapters. Each chapter will enrich your own work practice and, whatever your level of experience, you will gain from this book.

Remember, the more you do, and the more committed you are to advancing your work, the more you will see developments and improvements.

Be bold, be brave and take some risks but, above all, get started and do something!

SOME USEFUL TIPS

Keep your options open as long as possible – in other words, let the piece develop and evolve naturally.

Before starting each Skill Development exercise, read it through and gather together your materials.

Try not to have a view of how you want the piece to turn out. Be prepared to experiment, to explore and to enjoy the serendipity.

Relax and have some fun with your experimentation.

CHAPTER 1

Colour contrasts

Colour establishes the mood, underlines the artist's intentions and makes the initial impact. It is the main element of any work of art which immediately attracts the attention of the viewer and is central to its effectiveness.

Thus colour is a very powerful medium. If used skilfully, it can emphasise the personal feelings and ideas that the artist is trying to convey and it is an important factor in determining your individual style.

And so it's vital that you think positively about colour. Don't be idle. Choose the unpredictable colours. Always think beyond what is called 'local colour' (the grass is green, the sky is blue). Experimenting with colour is often a good starting point when we begin to push the boundaries of our visual artistic response to the world around us.

Ask the question

Are your first thoughts about your choice of colours the best? Will those colours convey how you feel about the subject matter?

Perhaps the grass may look better blue – why not? It's your work; there are no rights or wrongs. Colour is very personal and becomes so much more exciting when it is used unpredictably.

SO HOW CAN YOU USE COLOUR TO UNDERLINE YOUR THEME?

Colour can create a mood and a feeling. For the first exercise, we will select two contrasting feelings, 'energy' and 'tranquillity', to create a dynamic design and impact.

'Colour is my day-long obsession, joy and torment.'

Claude Monet

'Bar Chat'.
180 x 104 cm (71 x 41 in).
Strong contrasting colours convey the excitement of a chance meeting in this piece, constructed from unbleached calico (muslin) fabric, oil paint, printed and hand-dyed fabrics and hand and machine threads. The pre-stitched calico was painted white with an oil-based paint. Hand printed and commercial fabric areas were then stitched into place with hand and machine stitching.

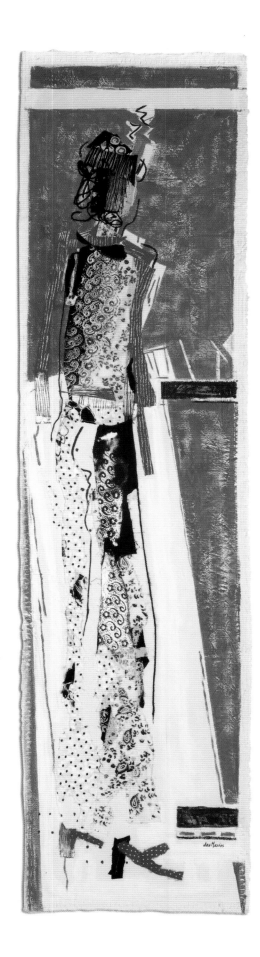

SKILL DEVELOPMENT 1

Energy and tranquillity

Energy can be generated by using optically opposing colour: red/green, purple/yellow or blue/orange. Green alongside red enhances the 'redness' of the red and vice versa. These are often referred to as complementary colours.

Tranquillity – what sort of colours come to mind? Different people will make different choices; perhaps a blue or cool green will be your choice?

AIM

To create a dramatic abstract design using energetic colours and contrasting them with calm, tranquil colours.

MATERIALS

- Coloured papers: A4 (Letter) is a good size

- **Energy:** choose two complementary colours; either red/green, blue/orange or yellow/purple

- **Tranquillity:** choose a quiet colour and texture; this will be your background paper

- Paper glue

- Scissors or scalpel and cutting board.

Examples of complementary colours:
Blue/Orange, Yellow/Purple, Red/Green.

METHOD

1 To enhance the feeling of energy, select a bold, strong shape with which to work. A hard-edged geometric shape, like a triangle, rectangle or square, would be perfect.

2 Cut several sizes of the same bold shape from one of the complementary colours, making sure you cut some very large and some very small.

3 Do not glue anything in place yet. Arrange the geometric shapes on the 'tranquil' A4 rectangle. Think of energy, movement and power. Why not work on the diagonal to add that extra frisson? Could they spill out over the background edge?

4 Now cut the same geometric shape from the other complementary colour. Think of the size you will need – a cluster of smaller shapes will create a very energetic focal point.

5 Placement is all-important. Move the shapes around until you find a startling position, one that will surprise the viewer.

6 Finally glue into place, pin up and step back to view from a distance.

Contrasting blue and orange triangles evolve into an energetic design against a calm blue background.

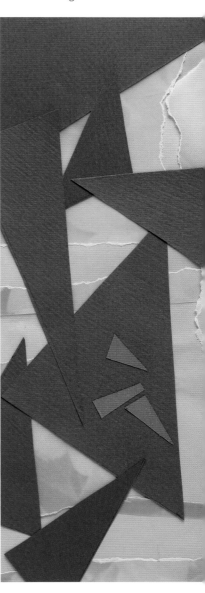

EXTENSION EXERCISES

1. Take the same starting point and extend by adding marks in coloured pencil or crayon and/or stitch to the 'energetic' area to enhance the impact.

2. Try a different geometric shape and an alternative colour option.

3. Now the risky part! Turn the paper collage over and cut from top to bottom with a curving line, adding another contrast.

4. Cut one more curving line across the collage.

5. Turn the paper collage back to the right side and arrange on a black background.

6. Let the cut collage shapes tumble over the background edges.

7. Glue in place. Pin up, step back and view the result from a distance.

Movement is created as paper and stitched triangles tumble out of the frame.

EXPLORING FURTHER
– YOUR PERSONAL WORK

Consider your own current work and ideas. Can these ideas of energy and tranquillity feature in your work? Is there an area that could be calmer where the eye can rest and relax?

Can you enliven a design by adding a splash of contrasting colour, creating a focal point? Can an area become more energetic with the addition of stitches and tiny scraps of fabric?

When you start a piece of work, always ask the question: Why am I using this colour? Is this the best choice?

Think positively about colour and your work will move forward. You will find that experimenting with colour and using unusual combinations will add a new dimension to your work.

Let's move on and create atmosphere, space and distance with colour.

A flash of orange provides a strong focal point on this pieced and patched textile.

Cold and warm

Cold colours contrasted with warm colours can create a dramatic sense of space and distance.

Warm colours, such as reds and oranges, will leap forward out of the picture, whereas cold colours like blues, greys and cool greens recede.

This device, called 'aerial perspective', is often used effectively by painters but a spatial awareness can sometimes be overlooked by textile artists as they concentrate on the two-dimensional aspect of their work.

Having a spatial awareness will lift your work from the ordinary to the exceptional.

AIM

To create 'aerial perspective' by using warm colours to move forward and cold colours to recede.

Note: The tone of the colours (how light or dark the colours are) is another important factor. Dark, strong colours will advance while light, paler colours will recede.

MATERIALS

- Paper – a good range of colours from warm to cold: reds, pinks, oranges, greens to light blues and greys
- White paper background, A4 (Letter)
- Paper glue.

'Mount Cook, New Zealand'. 24 x 15 cm (9 x 6 in). Watercolour on paper. In the foreground, warm orange reeds enhance the feeling of distance as the eye travels back to the cool snow covered peak of the mountain.

METHOD

A calm, static design will be developed using verticals and horizontals but no diagonals.

1   Tear one strip from each of your collection of coloured papers. Make some strips narrow and others wider.

2   Arrange the strips horizontally on the white background paper, placing the lightest/coolest colours at the top and gradually introducing the warmer bands of colour as you move down.

3   Make sure you cover all the white background paper with your wide and narrow strips.

4   Stand back from the collage and consider what is emerging. Do you need to change the sequence of colours? Perhaps you could tilt some of the strips to create an undulating landscape.

5   When the arrangement 'feels right', glue all the strips into place.

6   Pin up the final piece and, as you step further away, notice how the changes of colour create a feeling of space and distance.

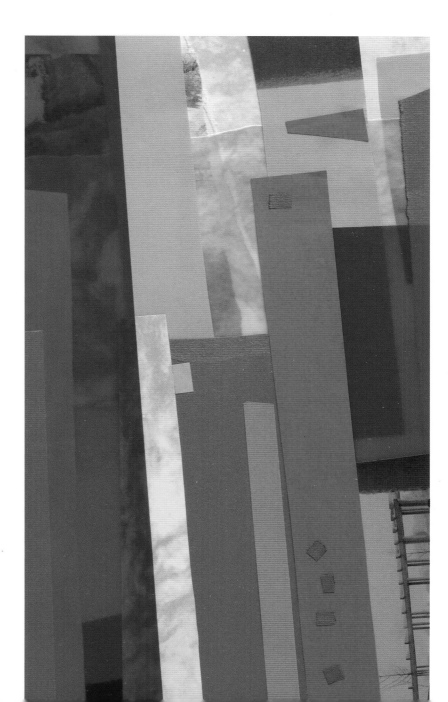

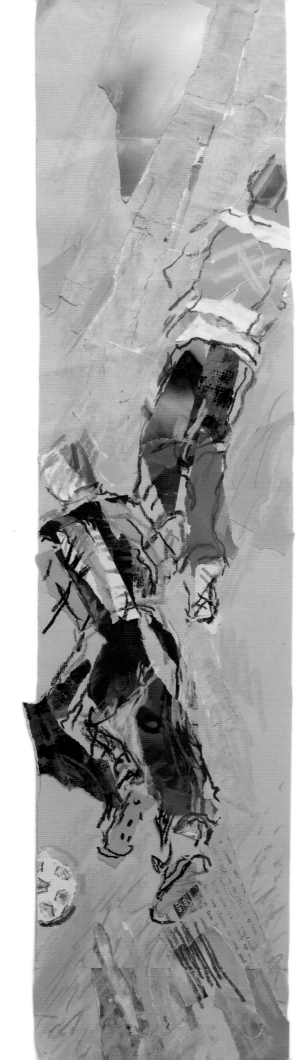

EXTENSION EXERCISES

1 An alternative is to work vertically. Imagine you are looking between buildings or trees. Forget 'local colour' – red trees are exciting! The aim here is to create a feeling of space by looking beyond the warm colours to the cooler distance.

2 Work with textured and hand-painted papers to add a surface interest to your collage.

A fluid design using diagonals creates movement and flux.

EXPLORING FURTHER – YOUR PERSONAL WORK

Skill Development 1 was based on diagonals to create an energetic design. Skill Development 2, using verticals and horizontals, produces a more stable, static composition.

WHEN BEGINNING A NEW PIECE OF WORK, YOUR FIRST QUESTION SHOULD BE:

Do you want a static, calm and stable composition? Does that suit your theme?

Verticals and horizontals will create that stability. Diagonals, on the other hand, contribute to the impression of action and movement. Consider whether your theme calls for some instability and flux.

SPATIAL AWARENESS: IS THIS REALLY A USEFUL TOOL IN TEXTILE ART WORK?

Not only can the cooler, lighter colours create distance but they can also establish passive areas where the eye can rest. Sometimes, in textile art work, there is a desire to over-decorate and 'busy' every area. The viewer needs restful as well as lively areas. Less can be more.

This static composition is based on verticals and horizontals.

SKILL DEVELOPMENT 3

Mood swings

We have mentioned that colour can emphasise the mood of a piece of work. This is where you will be able to use colour in a personal way as you interpret two contrasting emotions.

AIM

To use colour in a personal way and interpret some contrasting adjectives in two paper collages.

Choose from this list or select your own contrasting adjectives:

Cautious; rash

Mysterious; candid

Luxurious; meagre

Calm; excited

Serious; frivolous

Elegant; tasteless.

MATERIALS

- Coloured papers reflecting the chosen adjectives
- Pastels, crayons and/or inks
- Paper glue
- Scissors
- Backing paper, A4 (Letter) size.

'Fisherboys'.
150 x 92 cm (59 x 36 in).
Calm and peace prevail in this textile constructed from oil painted calico with commercial fabrics.

Above: 'Serious'.
Paper collage, Bridget Barber

Below: 'Frivolous'.
Paper collage, Bridget Barber

METHOD FOR EACH COLLAGE

1 One of your coloured papers may strongly suggest a mood or feeling. This could be the background for the collage. There is no right or wrong interpretation. Each person will have their own individual ideas. In the illustrated example, pink has been chosen as the background for 'frivolous' (page 19). Other equally frivolous colours make up the design.

2 Not only the colours but also your choice of shapes can reflect the adjectives. Will you cut or tear them? This can also have an impact on the outcome.

3 Weave, scatter, patch and piece your paper shapes onto the background paper.

4 When you feel that the arrangement reflects the mood, glue the pieces in place.

5 Add crayon, pastel and/or ink marks to underline the feelings evoked and draw the eye to important areas.

6 Place the two collages side by side to see the contrast.

EXTENSION EXERCISES

1 Different adjectives or tricky words like 'rush', 'drift' or 'fragility' can be explored.

2 Organise a group to do this exercise. It is fascinating to see how different your colleagues' reactions are.

Above: 'Rush'.
Paper collage, Jae Maries

Below: 'Rush'.
Paper collage, Valerie Riley

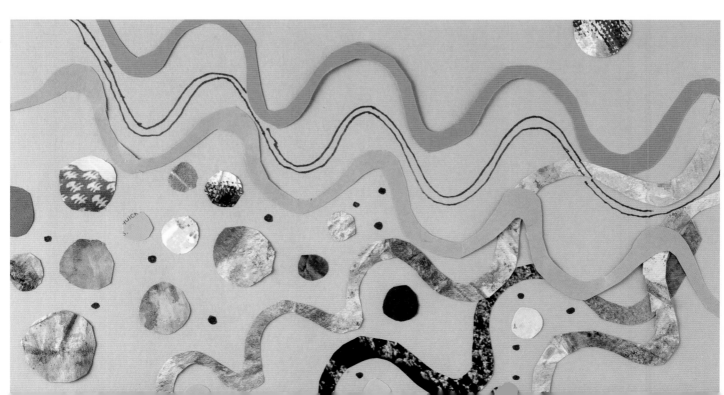

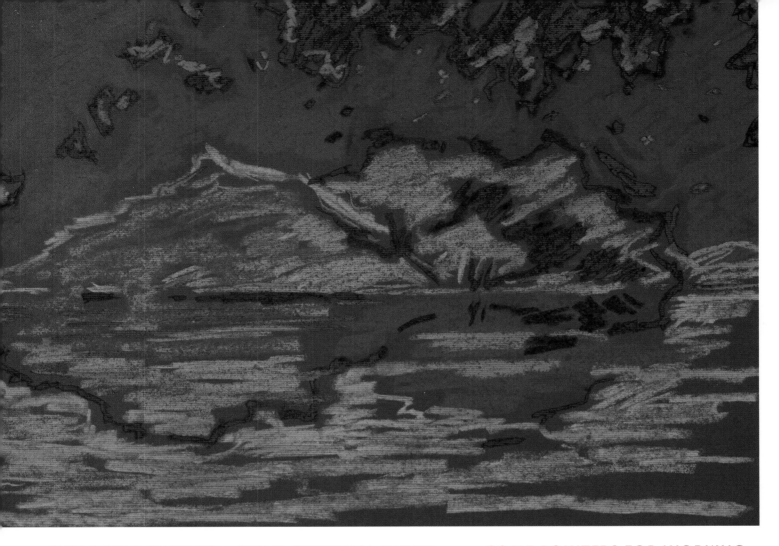

EXPLORING FURTHER – YOUR PERSONAL WORK

When you have an idea for new work, think about the atmosphere you want to create.

For instance, is your theme lively or contemplative? Pick an appropriate adjective to describe your theme. This will give your work an immediate personal slant and you will now be freer to select colours that are more innovative.

Be open-minded and have the confidence to move away from predictable, 'safe' colour choices.

As an example, your resource material may include photographs of a holiday scene. The atmosphere that you remember may have been relaxed or very exciting. So forget about 'local colour' (the grass is green, the sky is blue) and choose colours that reflect that mood. Be brave, take the plunge and mould the colours to underline your thoughts and memories. Be prepared to take some risks – you have nothing to lose but everything to gain.

SOME POINTERS FOR WORKING EFFECTIVELY WITH COLOUR

Always limit your colour palette.

Minimum colour equals maximum impact. Remember: you can use variations in tone, stretching the colour from its highest to its lowest notes.

Move away from local colour and be imaginative in your colour choices.

Take the leap and be provocative! Use the exact opposite to the colour you think you should use. You'll be surprised how very much more individual and exciting your work will become.

CHAPTER 2
Dynamic design

Good design is achieved when the artist thinks beyond his or her subject matter and considers more subtle elements, such as the marks that will be made, the shapes to be used and the rhythms and movement to create the composition.

These expressive forms, when used effectively, give all art work more impact, tension and conviction.

All these elements of design contribute to the work 'feeling right'.

Thus an awareness of the basic design concepts, along with a confident use of colour, will help you take possession of your idea and mould it to give your work more power and depth.

'I found I could say things
with colour and shapes that
I couldn't say any other way…
things I had no words for.'

Georgia O'Keeffe

'Empires Fall III'. 113 x 132 cm (44 x 52 in). This dramatic effect was achieved by using fabrics hand-dyed with water-based screen printing inks. These were patched and pieced together and enhanced with machine and hand stitching.

SKILL DEVELOPMENT 1

Conflicting scale

To add tension and dynamism to your work, having an awareness of the marks you make is hugely important. Believe it or not, small marks like hand stitches sprinkled on a simple fabric background can make a dominant statement if placed dramatically.

The conflicting scale of the fine line of a thread set against a large area of fabric is very powerful but sometimes that simple, direct statement can be submerged by overworking an area. It's very easy to do.

The following activity highlights the beauty of simple lines and their expressive power.

AIM

To produce a dramatic black-and-white design in paper using stitch marks to create added interest and diversity.

MATERIALS

- Black paper, 1 sheet, A4 (Letter) size
- White paper, 1 sheet, A4 (Letter) size
- Paper glue
- Threads – black and white
- Scissors
- Thimble
- Stiletto or darning needle
- Sewing machine (optional).

Hand and machine stitched lines contrast
with broad areas of printed and textured fabrics.

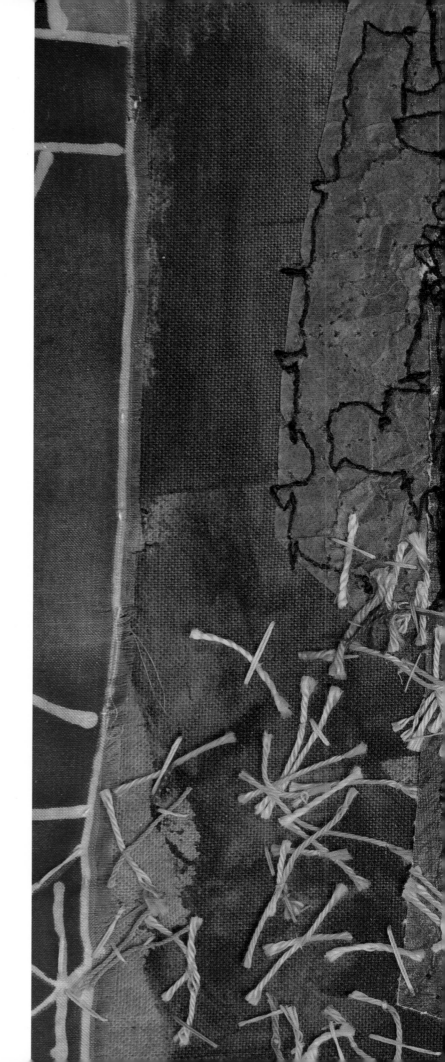

METHOD

Step 1

1   Make one cut diagonally right across the black sheet of paper.

2   Place the two shapes onto the white background. A white stripe has now been created. Is the stripe more dramatic thinner or wider?

3   Make another cut across one of the two black shapes. Place all three shapes back on the white background and move around to create dynamic areas of white and black.

4   Make one more cut but this time with a change of scale – a tiny nick works well.

5   Replace on the white background and become aware that white shapes are now emerging. They are just as vital as the black shapes. Every shape must have its own energy.

6   When you have a striking black-and-white design, glue in place.

Step 2

Now add that change of scale with stitch marks.

For hand stitching, consider running or back stitch. Machine stitching could include satin stitch or free straight stitch.

The stitches can straddle or follow the contours of the black-and-white forms. Use black thread on the white areas and white on the black paper.

Pin up the collage, stand back and see how these contrasting marks add another exciting dimension to the collage.

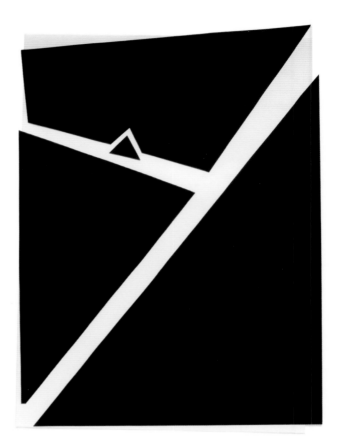

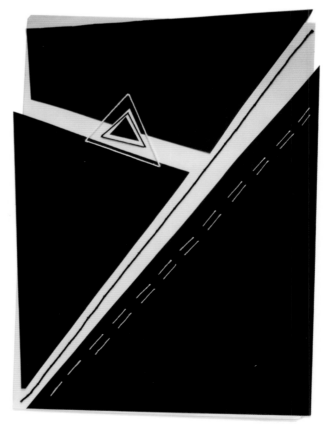

EXTENSION EXERCISES

1 Add extra stitches in a strong
   contrasting colour.

2 Work this exercise in fabric using
   different colour options: deep
   blue or red with a lighter tone.

EXPLORING FURTHER
– YOUR PERSONAL WORK

A change of scale is an important
element of design.

Enjoy the effectiveness of simple
stitch marks and the linear quality
of thread. It can be used to create
accents that help the viewer
navigate around the work.

Let's follow the linear theme now
and create a feeling of movement
with rhythmic, sinuous lines.

Simple lines help the viewer navigate
around this paper collage. Bridget Barber

SKILL DEVELOPMENT 2

Ebb and flow

AIM

To explore the contrasts of ebb and flow and create a structure in relief, using earth colours and rhythmical organic forms.

MATERIALS

- One piece of black plastic garden mesh (available at garden centres) minimum A4 (Letter) size.

- A collection of fabrics, papers, threads, yarns and string and/ or wire in earth colours – ochres, burnt umbers, siennas, chalks, mustards, charcoal etc.

- Large bodkin or darning needle (optional)

- Scissors

- Pins

- Black paper or black fabric for mounting the finished piece.

METHOD

1 Cut several thin strips of fabric and paper. They need to be narrow enough to be able to weave them in and out of the black garden mesh.

2 Begin weaving the strips, creating a flowing movement across the mesh, using a bodkin or your fingers. Keep the weaving loose and allow the fabric and paper strips to extend beyond the edges of the mesh as this will add to the organic sense of growth.

3 When you have built up the textured structure, think about adding the strings, threads, yarns and/or wire. These can create long tendril-like forms or suggest small 'twigs' that spurt out from the centre of the structure.

4 The piece is now ready to be mounted onto the black paper or fabric but first cut away any excess mesh. Then twist or manipulate your organic structure to enhance the movement of the piece. Pin in place.

5 Hand stitch the organic form onto the background with black thread.

Right: A woven structure using Earth Colours. Bridget Barber

Left: A collection of Earth Colours.

EXTENSION EXERCISES

1   Imagine the flight of a bird as it flits from
    branch to ground then to bird feeder.
    On paper or fabric, draw or stitch that
    movement, creating a continuous line.

2   Select a musical phrase. Listen to the
    extract of music several times then,
    taking paper and paint or charcoal,
    interpret the extract in marks and
    scribbles as you listen. Think about the
    rhythm, the accents and the colours.
    Make marks on paper or fabric to
    capture the mood of the piece.

'City Streets'. 112 x 88 cm (44 x 34 in).
Diagonal lines help move the eye through this piece of
work. Here, the base fabric was prepared as before and
oil painted before applying textured fabric scraps, when
dry, with hand and machine stitching.

EXPLORING FURTHER
– YOUR PERSONAL WORK

Rhythmic patterns in a composition create
pathways for the eye to move smoothly
around the work.

Every part of a piece of work must be
considered as each section contributes to
its overall harmony. Sometimes it's difficult
to 'stand outside' your own piece of work
and see it objectively. A tried and tested
way of getting a fresh view is to look at
the reverse image in a mirror. Suddenly you
become aware of changes that need to be
made to improve the harmony and impact
of the work.

'City Streets' (detail).
The homeless figure
is isolated within a
threatening environment
and is hurrying to find a
place of safety.

SKILL DEVELOPMENT 3

Friction in form

The exercises so far have dealt with abstract basic design concepts: colour, mark making and scale. Let's look at a method of working from a group of everyday objects, concentrating on the contrasting forms. This will encourage you to become more flexible in your own work and to welcome the unexpected.

AIM

To work in paper and create a design from an arrangement of objects using stitch – either hand or machine – to add some details in a linear form.

MATERIALS

- A collection of simple objects
- Coloured paper – choose one colour from the objects and then, ignoring all other colours, select two different colours that harmonise with your first choice (this is the first break from the predictable)
- Paper glue
- White background paper, A4 (Letter) size
- Scissors
- Needles – darning or stiletto
- Sewing machine (optional)
- Hand stitching threads.

A collection of objects for use as inspiration for a paper collage design.

METHOD

Step 1

1 Place the objects on a table. Don't worry about the arrangement. We're looking at the forms of the objects.

2 Select one of the coloured papers and tear or cut out the shape of the largest forms from the still life. Place this torn shape onto the white background paper. Make sure you keep the torn negative shape.

3 Tear out another shape from the group of objects using a different coloured paper. Place this on the white background paper, again keeping the negative shape.

4 Now look to see how you can use the negative shapes. These are useful for filling in the background. Your aim is to cover all the white paper using the positive and negative shapes. Tear out more shapes if you need them.

5 As you arrange the paper shapes, remember that you can overlap, invert or turn them sideways. Don't worry if you do not use every object in the still life.

6 When you have a pleasing design, glue in place.

Step 2

Now we will add the contrasting form as a line or contour.

1 From the still life objects, choose a form, pattern or detail that you have not yet used. Select a strong contrasting colour thread and 'float' the shape of the object or pattern over the paper collage, using the thread to draw the contour thus adding a second 'layer' to the design. Think about the placement and size of the shape. You may wish to make it larger in scale.

Torn paper shapes making use of the positive and negative forms.

2 Stitch the outline contour in place. Consider hand couching, back or chain stitch, or use the sewing machine with free straight stitch.

3 Add more outline forms if you wish and pin up when complete to consider the final composition.

You will have achieved a piece of work that represents the group of objects without being a slave to the proportions, colour or arrangement. The contrast between the solid forms and contours adds a new dimension to the collage.

EXTENSION EXERCISES

1 This exercise would translate well into fabric. A different colour scheme could be your starting point.

2 A small series could be developed in fabric using the same still life objects. The three colours could have a different emphasis in each design with different contrasting threads. The finished pieces would hang one below another.

EXPLORING FURTHER – YOUR PERSONAL WORK

This method of designing, using solid forms and then overlaying with the outlines of other related shapes, is a great way of breaking away from the traditional approach to representational art work. Not only can you contrast positive and negative forms but you can also be flexible over the proportions and the scale of the objects.

Left: Paper collage with the pattern from the tablecloth hand stitched across the piece.

Three more designs taken from the still life objects.

CHAPTER 3

Material bravura

When you start to explore the world of innovative textile art, the one aspect that strikes you immediately is the vast range materials that are employed – everything from fabrics to plastics and paper to wood, metal and ceramics.

All can be used to create amazing textural contrasts – smooth/rough, hard/soft, light/heavy – and the fabrics themselves can be manipulated, cut, torn, stitched and stiffened to create exciting surface interest.

But where to start?

Here is an opportunity to experiment with some simple materials and break away from the conventional.

'Have no fear of perfection. You'll never reach it.'

Salvador Dali

A photographic and fabric montage recalling a French garden.

SKILL DEVELOPMENT 1

Sheen and matt

These two surface textures contrast well with each other, each moderating the character of the other to form a harmony. Too much sheen and the work looks destined for the glossy magazine, too matt and it can become dull.

We will be working with shiny photographs and juxtaposing them with matt fabric. Most people have access to photographic prints and in many cases they will be the main resource from which ideas and themes evolve into future work. So this is a good way to use them directly.

AIM

To combine photographs that have a linking theme with fabrics and to expand the atmosphere and feelings behind the photographs.

MATERIALS

- Three or four photographs with an underlying connection, for example location, family or time. These will be torn up, so use nothing precious (or scan them first and print out on glossy photographic paper)

- A collection of fabrics that reflect the atmosphere of the photographs

- Darning needle

- Jeans needle for the sewing machine

- Threads – machine and hand

- Backing fabric – thin cotton

- Sewing machine (optional).

Contrasting materials of paper, print and fabric are combined to create a wistful montage of a childhood long past.

METHOD

1 Collect fabrics and threads that empathise with the photographs. Memories could suggest faded colours and worn fabrics. Wonderful holiday shots perhaps call for vibrant colours and strong prints. Garden photos could reflect the seasons.

2 Tear or cut out interesting parts of the photographs, keeping the torn remnants.

3 Begin to arrange the photographic fragments onto your backing fabric with your fragment scraps. This could follow several formats. For example, old photos could follow a linear, meandering form suggesting a quiet reflective path. Holiday snaps could be much more energetic, placed on the diagonal with bold fabric strips interspersed.

4 When the work 'feels right', select hand or machine threads to attach the pieces to the background fabric. Use a thick machine needle (jeans type) to penetrate the photographic paper, or a darning needle and thimble for hand stitching.

5 Pin up your work and look at it from a distance. Does your choice of fabric echo the mood of the photographs? Have you been able to combine the two contrasting textures effectively?

Photographs stitch remarkably well and the challenge is to make a smooth transition from the sheen of the photograph to the matt and textured feel of the fabrics. In the finished sample some photographic prints have been used (see the Extension exercise for details).

Printing on silk organza.

EXTENSION EXERCISE

Photographs can easily be transferred onto very fine fabric using a photocopier. The light-fast quality of the photocopier inks is generally poor so fading may occur over time but this method is a wonderful way to achieve delicate prints.

MATERIALS

- Very fine fabric – silk organza, fine cotton lawn
- Typing paper, A4 (Letter) size.

METHOD

1 Cut the fine fabric to A4 size.

2 Attach to A4 typing paper with double-sided sticky tape all around the edges.

3 Put the photograph to be copied in the photocopier and feed the A4 sheet with the thin fabric attached through the machine. Make sure there aren't any loose ends that could get caught in the machine.

4 Hey presto! You will have the image printed onto fine gauze. These delicate images can fit beautifully into textile work by subtly suggesting a location or image of a person.

5 Photographic details of flowers can be torn or cut out and the frame created from fabric scraps. The cloth fragments and stitching could reflect the flower colours and season of the year.

If you don't have access to a photocopier, try the Extravaganza fabric for inkjet printers.

Left: Design ideas using
cut-up photographs.

Below: Using 'L' shapes to crop
and intensify a composition.

EXPLORING FURTHER
– YOUR PERSONAL WORK

The simple act of cutting up photographs is an effective design tool, particularly if you have several images of one theme. The strips can be grouped together and will represent an all-round view of the subject matter. The innovative design can then be traced, enlarged and translated into fabric and thread.

Always be prepared to experiment with your resource material by cropping, cutting up and re-piecing. By severely cropping the photographs vertically or horizontally, you arrive at a tighter, more dynamic design.

If the original photographs are precious then use tracing paper or reproduce them on a photocopier.

Static and fluid

As soon as you start working with contrasting materials, you can readily move into three dimensions. The contrast between static forms and fluid materials will present opportunities for making free-standing objects as well as bringing a tension to the work as the eye moves from stiffness to flexibility.

AIM

To make a simple four-sided open vessel from unbleached calico (muslin in the USA), laced together with paper string. The rigid textured sides of the vessel will contrast with the flexibility of the paper string.

MATERIALS

- Unbleached calico (muslin)
- White or cream thread – crochet cotton #8 or finer
- Needle
- Scissors
- Stiletto or darning needle
- White paper string – see Suppliers
- PVA
- Plastic for covering work surface
- 2.5 cm (1 in) household paintbrush.

METHOD

1 Tear four rectangles 10 x 20 cm (4 x 8 in) from the calico and a fifth square for the base 12 x 12 cm (4¾ x 4¾ in). Fray all the edges a little to create an attractive soft edge. The tearing may stretch the edges of the torn shapes. To restore them, spray water on the edges and allow to dry.

2 To add texture and surface interest to the calico sides, first apply some fine scrim. This can extend beyond the top of the vessel, creating an upwards lift. Then add hand and/or machine stitching to each side panel, varying the direction of the stitches to add pattern to the textured surface. Keep the back tidy or consider lining the vessel later. Stitch options: running or herringbone stitch, seeding or couched threads with hand or machine stitching.

Right: Materials including calico, thread, paper string, PVA. Brush and stiletto also shown.

Left: A free-standing vessel of calico stiffened with PVA and laced together with paper string.

3 Cover your work surface with a plastic sheet. Place the pre-stitched calico rectangles and the square base face-up on the plastic sheet.

4 Using the paintbrush, spread neat PVA evenly over each calico shape. At this point you can apply some lines of paper string to extend beyond the top of the vessel to create the contrast with flowing movement. Leave to dry. This could take an hour or more. Make sure you wash your brush immediately or it will harden.

5 When thoroughly dry, peel the stiffened squares off the plastic sheet.

6 Now to make the holes along all the edges for lacing the sides together. On a piece of paper, measure out the placement of the holes. They should be about 1 cm (½ in) in from the edge for the first hole and 2.5 cm (1 in) from the top. Make five holes with a gap of 4 cm (1½ in) between each. Place the template along one of the short edges of the rectangle and, using a stiletto or thick darning needle, pierce through the paper into the calico. Repeat along all the long sides. Enlarge each hole for threading through the string.

7 The sides are now ready to be laced together. Cut four 80 cm (31½ in) lengths of paper string.

Two stitched and stiffened calico rectangles laced together with paper string.

8 To join two sides together, thread the string through the two bottom holes and lace to the top. Tie loosely to secure it. Continue to join the other three sides to form the vessel.

9 To fix the base square, fold in 1 cm (½ in) turning on each of the four sides. Mitre the corners. Paint PVA on the turnings, invert the vessel and position the base. Glue in place and hold in position with paper-clips until firmly adhered. The contrast between the stiffened calico and the sinuous threads will now be apparent. Cut back the paper string ties to the length you think feels right. (See photograph on page 42.)

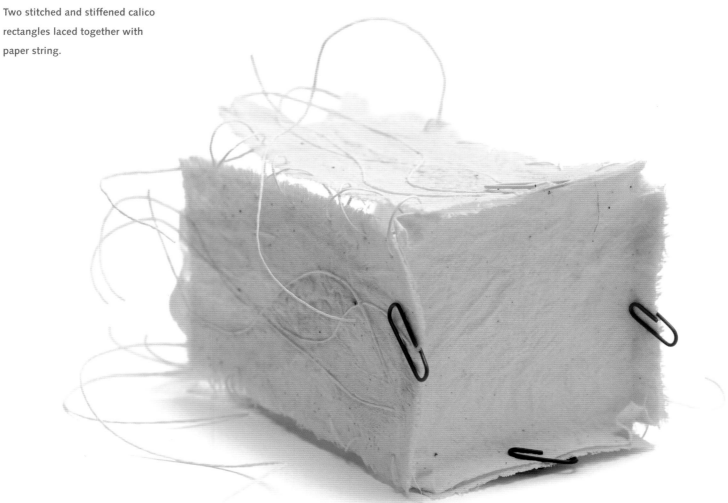

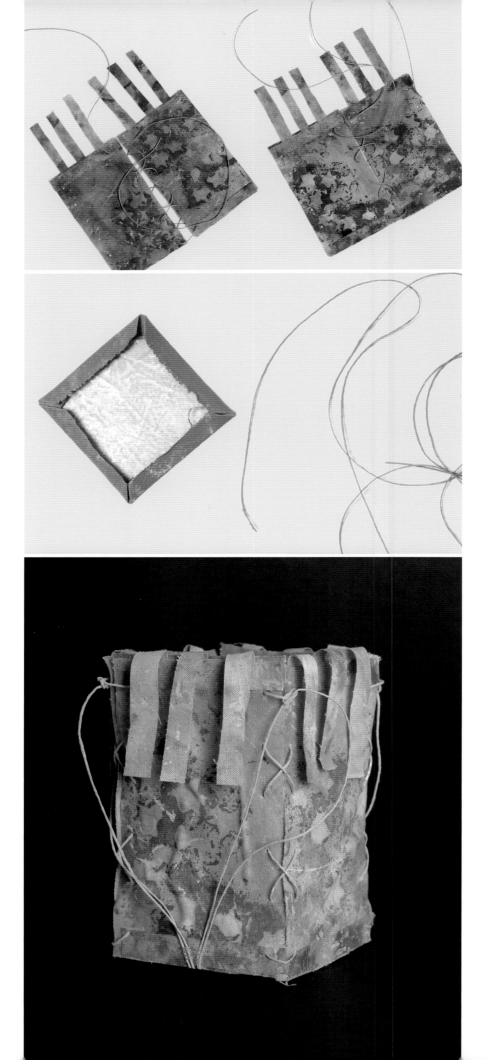

EXTENSION EXERCISES

1   As well as varying the proportions of the calico sides, other materials can be explored. PVA can stiffen pre-painted or dyed fabrics. Wire mesh or handmade papers can be substituted for the calico. The sides can be laced together with ribbons, thread or fabric strips.

2   To form rigid linear patterns, the calico can be pleated, tucked or smocked before applying the PVA.

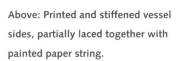

Above: Printed and stiffened vessel sides, partially laced together with painted paper string.

Below: Finished vessel.

EXPLORING FURTHER
– YOUR PERSONAL WORK

Stiffening fabric with PVA can extend your artistic vocabulary in an immediate way. It frees you from the flat two-dimensional surface and encourages your work to develop sculpturally.

These three-dimensional spiral forms were constructed from painted and stiffened calico and paper. Painted kebab sticks add rigidity.

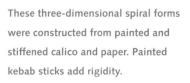

SKILL DEVELOPMENT 3

Natural and synthetic

Here are two contrasts that we come across in everyday life although there is often the desire to use natural materials rather than synthetic fibres such as nylon, acetate and plastic. However, we are looking for the dramatic so, putting our prejudices to one side, let's give it a go.

AIM

To produce a small hanging using cellophane, shrink-wrapped to trap natural objects such as petals and leaves.

MATERIALS

- Florist's cellophane
- Non-stick baking parchment
- Petals and leaves
- Hand embroidery threads – colour to complement the flower or leaf colour
- Iron and ironing board.

METHOD

1   Make a small collection of petals, leaves and some strands of embroidery threads.

2   Cut out two large sheets of baking parchment and two lengths of cellophane, one approximately 15 x 40 cm (6 x 16 in) and the other 15 x 30 cm (6 x 12 in). Round off the corners of both.

3   Place one of the sheets of baking parchment on the ironing board and then the shorter sheet of cellophane on top.

4   Now arrange the threads, petals and leaves in the centre of the cellophane. Allow the threads to extend beyond the cellophane. These can be used to hang the piece later.

5   Complete the sandwich with the longer sheet of cellophane and then the second sheet of baking parchment.

6   Press firmly with the hot iron for 2–3 seconds on the baking parchment sandwich. The heat from the iron will make the cellophane shrink, trapping the contents.

7   Allow to cool and peel off the cellophane. There will be some condensation from the organic matter but that will evaporate.

The results can be unpredictable but that's the fun of it.

Heat-shrunk cellophane with trapped petals, leaves and threads for suspending the sample.

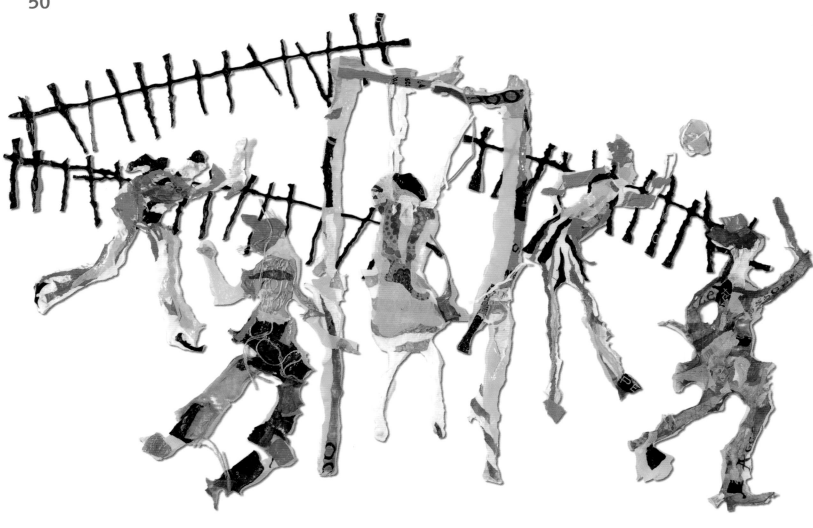

EXTENSION EXERCISES

1 Heat-shrinking can also be applied to plastic bags, resulting in material that is tough enough to be stitched into and painted with acrylic paint. The thinnest bags shrink rapidly whereas thicker ones shrink less.

2 A lively series can be developed by creating quirky figures and developing a storyline, perhaps centred on children playing in the street or on the swings in the park.

HEALTH AND SAFETY

Wear an appropriate mask for this process.

EXPLORING FURTHER – YOUR PERSONAL WORK

The concept of working in a series is a valuable method of developing your work. Could your own ideas and themes suggest a series?

Instead of putting everything into one piece of art work, perhaps the idea could grow into three or four individual pieces with a linking theme.

Different aspects of an event or scene could emerge as the series develops.

Working in this way demands a focused approach. You will think more deeply about your themes and ideas, and your resulting work will have a more personal impact.

'The Playground'. Heat-shrunk plastic shopping bags create lively figures suitable for a series of work.

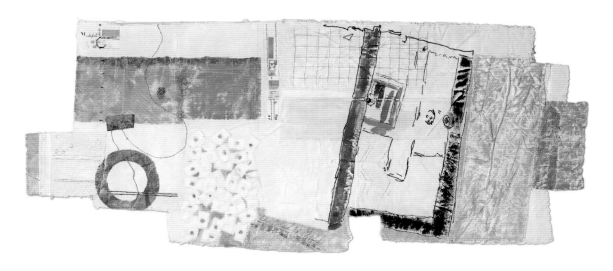

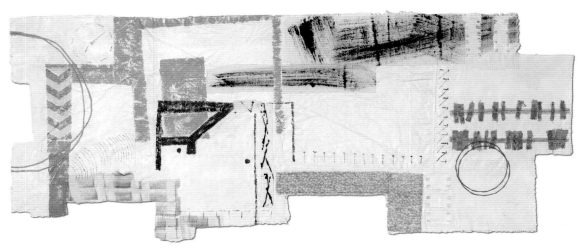

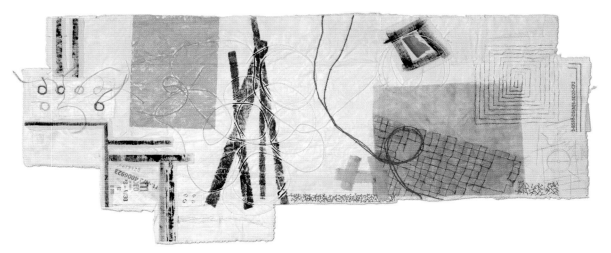

'Site Development Series IV, V, VI'.
120 x 65 cm (47 x 25 in)
This series follows the building of a
new house from the planning stage,
through the ground-works, to the
interior development. The materials
used were unbleached calico (muslin),
oil paint, printed fabrics, hand and
machine threads. These were pre-
stitched and patched together, then
prepared to take oil paint. Details
were then painted in and printed
fabrics, paper and other materials
added, together with hand and
machine stitching.

CHAPTER 4

Opposing processes

LET'S RECAP

We first explored how to use colour to draw out your feelings and emotions and create a visual impact. Then certain aspects of design were investigated to assist you in expressing your ideas more effectively.

In Chapter 3, Material bravura, we looked at the potential of contrasting fabrics with other materials so that the diversity and content of your work can be increased.

Now we reach the actual making of the work, and similar questions arise. Which techniques can you use to demonstrate your passion about your subject matter? Which materials best reflect the theme you are trying to portray?

Your choice of techniques is, to a large part, down to personal taste. Maybe you can't stand the messiness of paint and dye, or veer away from the precision of gold work and delicate stitching. However, you may have been using the same technique for some time, so it's good to try something different. It may just kick-start you in a new, exciting direction.

In this chapter we will be experimenting with constructed textiles, weaving and wrapping, and manipulated fabrics and stitch. You will have the opportunity to include your own favourite techniques, adding to the diversity.

'A lot of it is experimental, spontaneous. It's knocking about in the studio and bumping into things.'

Richard Prince

SKILL DEVELOPMENT 1

Knotting and knitting

We will start with knotting, creating an open grid. Knitting, a contrasting technique, will be used to fill part of the grid.

AIM

To create a knotted grid and suspend within it a patchwork of small knitted samples.

A limited colour scheme will be chosen as this is essential to creating a cohesive piece of art work.

Step 1 Knotting

MATERIALS

- Paper string, white or coloured
- Masking tape
- Needles, pins, scissors
- Firm flat board 33 x 25 cm (13 x 10 in) approx.

METHOD

1 Cut the paper string into nine lengths of 45 cm (18 in) each.

2 Take four lengths of string and attach them, with masking tape, to the top of your flat board, 5 cm (2 in) apart.

3 Straighten the string lines and attach the other ends loosely to the working surface with masking tape. There must be enough slack within the string lines to be able to knot the traversing threads.

4 Now take one of the remaining five lengths and, starting 5 cm (2 in) down from the masking tape, knot it to the first vertical string with a simple slip knot, leaving a 5 cm (2 in) end.

5 Move across to the next vertical string and repeat the knotting. Carry on and knot the traversing string to all four vertical strings.

6 Now take the second length of string and knot across the next line about 5 cm (2 in) below the first row and so on until you have completed the grid. Tighten all the knots but do not worry if the squares are a little irregular. You will make twelve squares. Trim off any extra-long ends.

7 At this point, you can add some supplementary knotting within one or two of the squares using the paper string, thread or ribbon.

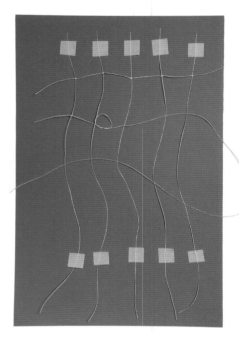

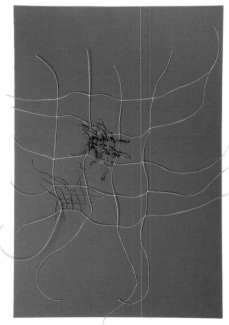

Step 2 Knitting

AIM

To knit small squares to suspend within the knotted grid but limiting the colours to achieve a pleasing harmony (see Further Reading, page 80 for books on knitting).

MATERIALS

- A variety of threads, fabric strips, crochet cotton, wools, paper string and/or wire
- Knitting needles
- Crochet hook.

METHOD

1 Knit a small square in any stitch, choosing one of your selected threads. Plain, pearl or moss stitch will work well. Eight stitches knitted with 5 mm needles will produce a square of about the right size. Try experimenting with different-sized needles and unusual materials.

2 Complete several patches and leave to one side.

3 An option, at this point, is to do some more knotting within the grid, as shown in the sample. Tape down the loose ends of the large grid to give stability and knot within one or two squares, tying the threads to the large knotted grid.

4 Now attach the knitted squares to the grid by hand using a matching thread.

5 Feel free to dye the string, and add some printed fabric pieces and crocheted patches to the grid for variety and interest.

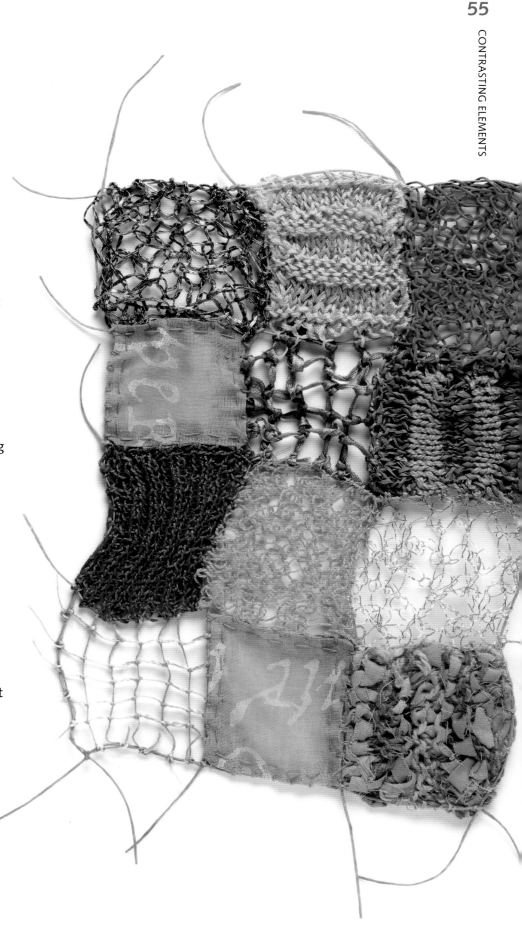

EXTENSION EXERCISE

The second sampler shows a knotted grid that had been painted first. Then a variety of patches were suspended in the grid. Other forms of constructed textiles were added, like lace, weaving, crochet and felt.

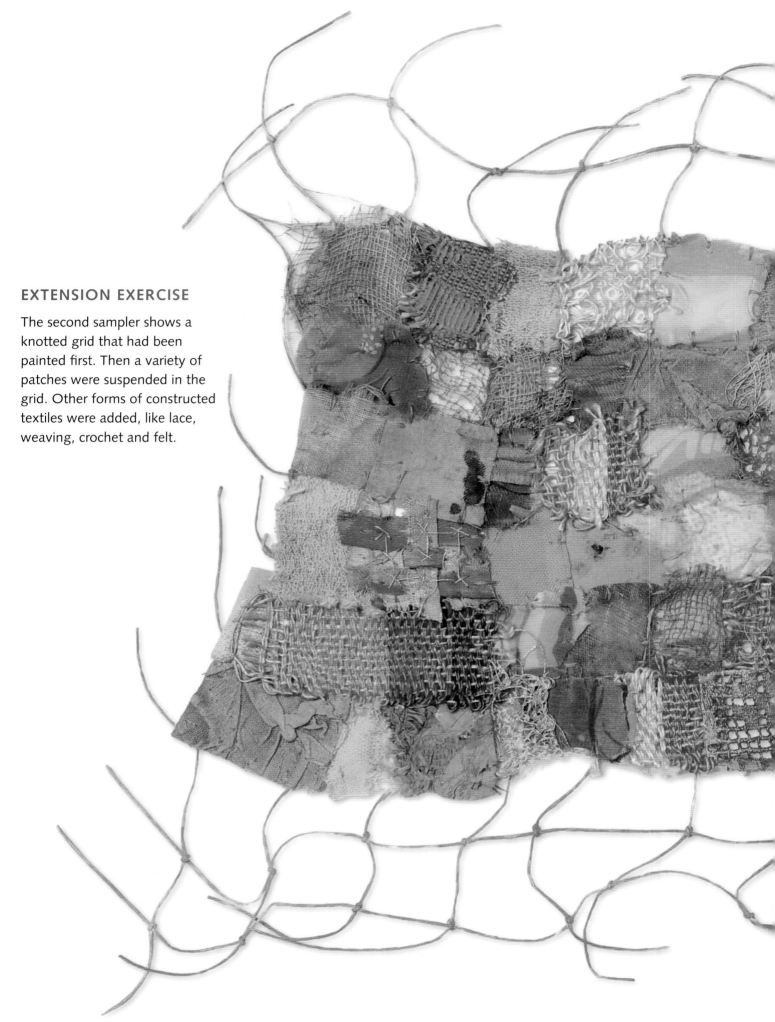

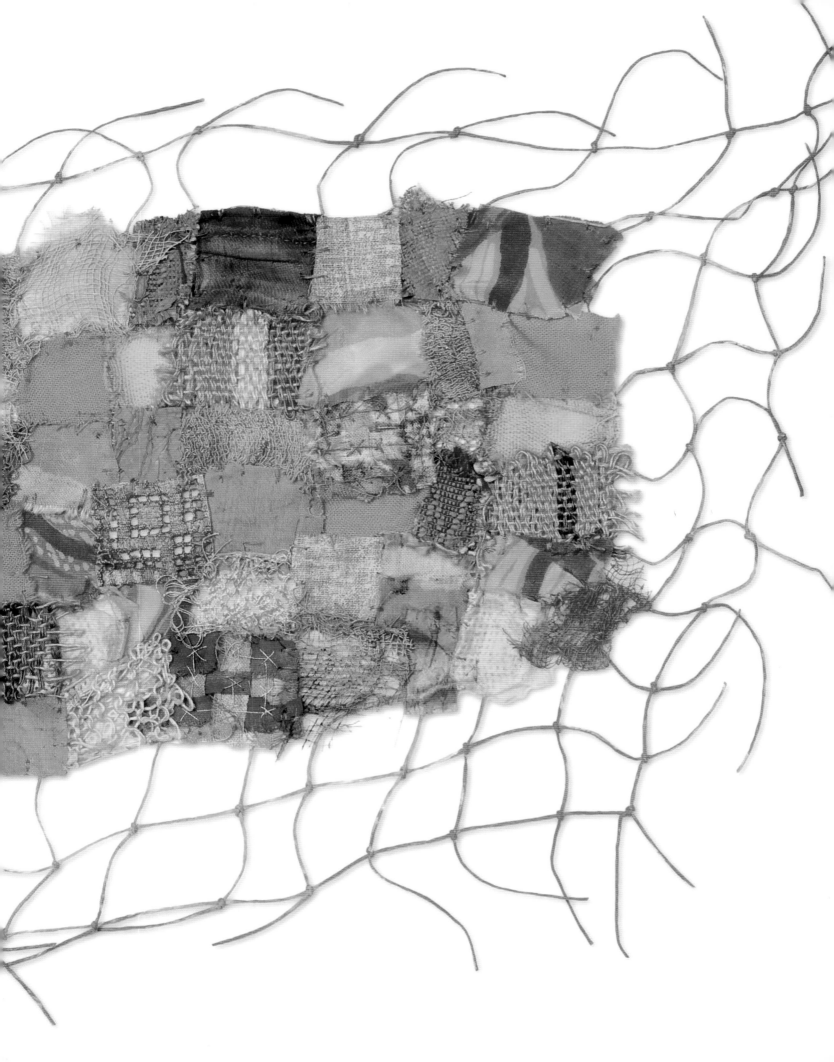

SKILL DEVELOPMENT 2

Wrapping and weaving

AIM

To contrast a decorative wrapped framework with the fluid lines of loosely woven panels.

Step 1 Wrapping

This is a flexible technique that can be used to add colour and pattern to a variety of rigid sticks, rods or straws. In this task, wrapping is used to decorate kebab sticks, creating a firm structure to support small woven panels.

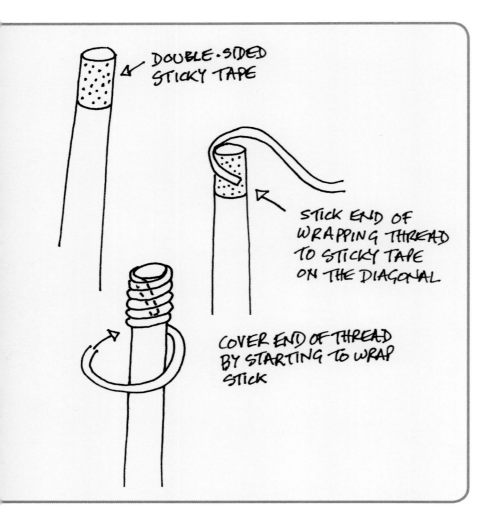

MATERIALS

- Straws, kebab or plant support sticks or acrylic rods

- Long lengths of threads – choose an attractive colour harmony (space-dyed threads are very effective and were used in the illustrated sample)

- Double-sided sticky tape

- Scissors.

METHOD

1 Cut a narrow strip of double-sided sticky tape and attach it, circling the very top of one of the sticks.

2 Begin to wrap the stick by attaching the thread to the sticky tape at a downward angle (see diagram). Now wrap the thread around the top of the stick, covering the cut end as you move down the stick. The thread needs to be long enough to reach the end of the stick because it is difficult to join threads along the stick. If you do need to add another thread then repeat the starting method at the top of the stick. As you are wrapping, make sure there are no gaps between the threads. Continue until the whole stick is covered.

3 To secure the thread at the end, attach to another piece of sticky tape at the base of the stick and wrap over it until you have covered the stick. Cut off the loose end.

4 Continue to wrap all eight sticks, changing the colours of the threads if required.

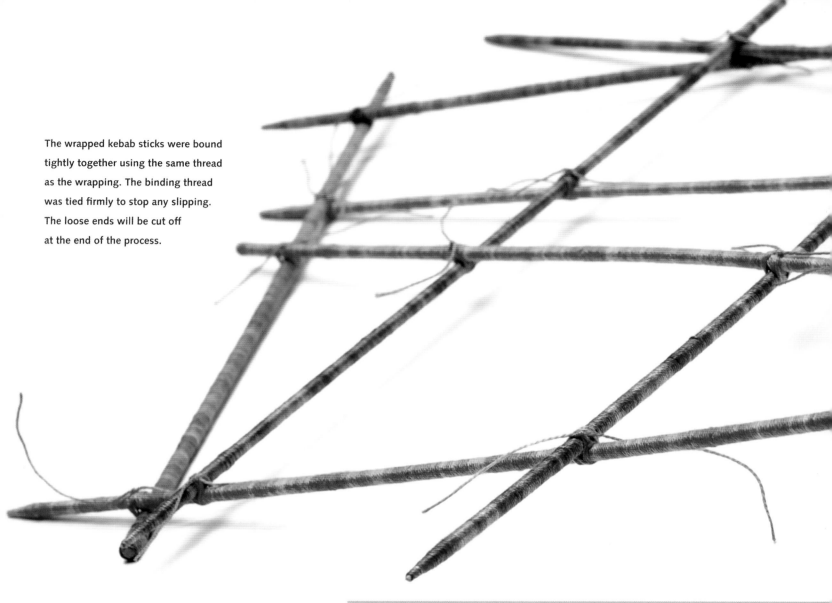

The wrapped kebab sticks were bound tightly together using the same thread as the wrapping. The binding thread was tied firmly to stop any slipping. The loose ends will be cut off at the end of the process.

TO MAKE A RIGID STRUCTURE

1 Place the wrapped sticks on a flat surface in a pattern to create several four-sided rectangles. These can be irregular rectangles, giving the grid extra dynamism.

2 When you have achieved a good arrangement, tie or bind the sticks together at the intersections. Make sure any knots are at the back of the grid. As you join the wrapped sticks together, you may be able to twist the structure so that it is no longer flat.

Now you are ready to weave some panels.

Above: Selected areas were prepared for weaving by winding a warp thread firmly across two sides of the selected area.

Step 2 Weaving

This is another form of constructed textile that we will be exploring in its most basic but effective format.

In weaving, the weft goes from left to right and the warp goes from top to bottom.

The phrase 'weft to wite' amuses me and helps me distinguish the two.

MATERIALS

A selection of threads, wools, strips of fabric within your chosen colour scheme. Bodkin (optional).

METHOD

1   Select a rectangle to work in and begin to thread up the warp by tying one end of the warp thread to the top wrapped stick on the left-hand side. Wrap the thread around the frame from top to bottom. Space the warp threads depending on the thickness of the thread or wool – about 1 cm (½ in) apart if you are using a wide warp but less if it is thinner. Keep the warp very taut. The tension of the wrapped framework will keep it in place. When you have your warp firmly wrapped on the frame, tie the end securely.

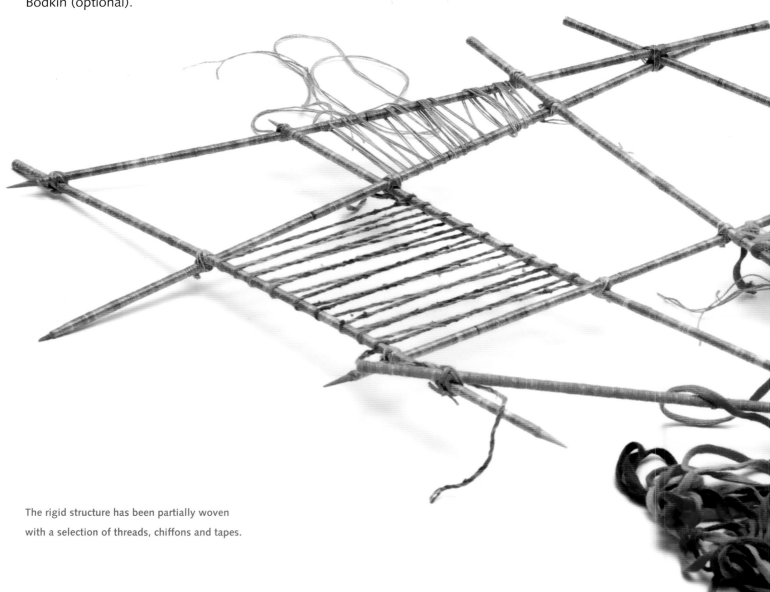

The rigid structure has been partially woven
with a selection of threads, chiffons and tapes.

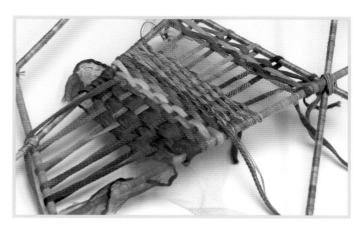

2 Now you can begin to weave the weft, selecting either wools, yarns or strips of fabric. The fabric strips need to be narrow and can be crunched up as you weave. Tie a knot at the beginning of the row and weave across using your fingers or a bodkin. At the end of the row, weave around the wrapped framework and return, weaving as many rows as you wish. To finish, secure with another knot. When you've completed the weaving, neaten the loose ends by either sewing or weaving them back into the constructed textile.

3 Decide which other areas you wish to weave. You may decide to leave the warp threads without any weaving or, perhaps, fill in with some fabric patches to add variety to the piece of work.

EXTENSION EXERCISES

1 Both processes – wrapping and weaving – can be explored further by using a variety of different materials; wrapped twigs could create a more fluid, organic grid and plastic strips or paper can be used for the weaving.

2 The rigid wrapped structure could be used to suspend photographs or found objects.

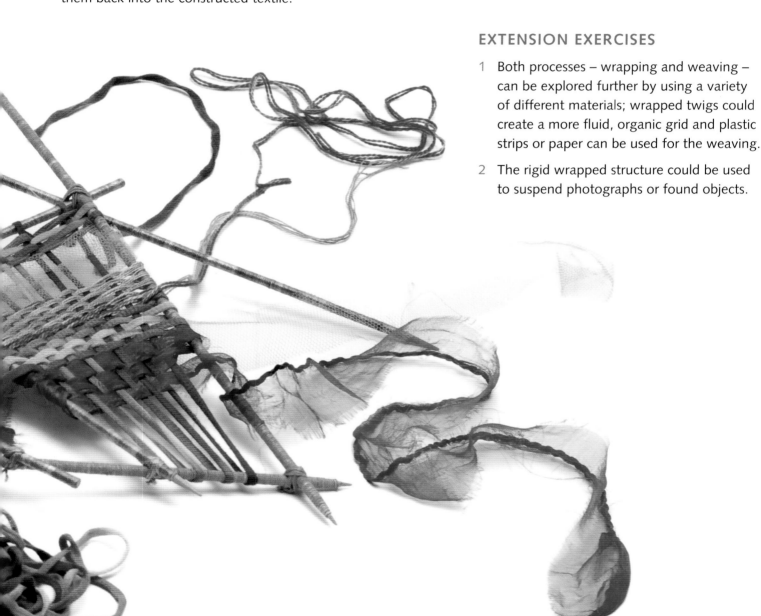

SKILL DEVELOPMENT 3

Manipulated fabric and stitch

The term 'manipulated fabric' covers such techniques as layering, appliqué, pleating, tucking, quilting etc.

AIM

To explore the process of layering and appliqué.

To extend the cut-back techniques with added stitch for surface decoration to form the contrast.

Step 1 Making the layers

1 Choose four colours from light to dark that make a pleasing colour harmony.

2 Select a variety of fabrics within the colour range. These can be printed and hand-dyed fabrics. Chiffons, gauzes and thin cottons can be used later to add surface texture to the middle layers.

3 Decide on the sequence of colours and cut one square approximately 25 x 25 cm (10 x 10 in) for the top layer. Cut another square the same size, from a different fabric, for the bottom layer.

4 For the two central layers, we will make up two squares from fabrics patched together. To make the patched layers, work like this:

   - Cut two squares from your remaining fabrics and use these as the backing fabric.

   - Add strips and patches of similar-coloured fabric, such as chiffons and gauzes.

   - Pin these in place and machine or hand stitch the added pieces into place.

You should now have four squares. The middle two are the ones with applied fabric.

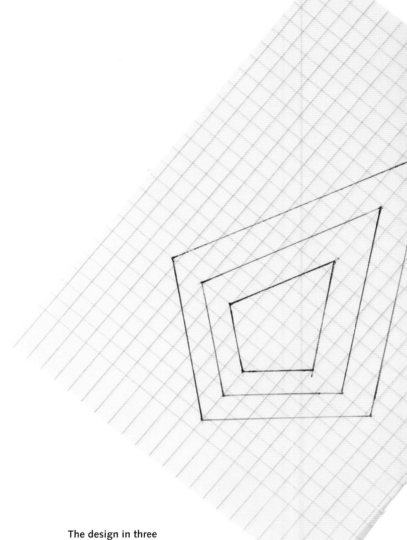

The design in three reducing sizes was drawn onto graph paper.

Step 2 Cut-away appliqué

1 Take the four squares of fabric and form a layered sandwich. Pin them together at the top only.

2 Choose a shape to work with and cut three templates, each decreasing in size. The largest diamond shown in the sample is 14 x 10 cm (5½ x 4 in). Pin the largest template slightly off-centre on the top layer and cut out the shape. Keep the cut-out piece to one side.

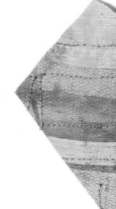

The two largest shapes have
been cut out from the top two
layers of the four layers of fabric.
The cut-out shapes are kept for use later.

3 Repeat the process. With the top layer in place, pin the next template to the second layer. Then fold back the top layer of fabric and cut out the shape from the second layer. Retain the cut-out piece. Then use the smallest template for the third layer of fabric. Keep this cut-out shape as well. This will result in the shape (decreasing in size) having been cut out in the same place on all three layers.

4 Leave the bottom layer solid. Don't worry about the edges at this stage. They can either be frayed out or stabilised with machine or hand stitching later.

Now you can have some fun!

5 Unpin the four layers, keeping them in the same sequence, and shift them around to create a dramatic new pattern.

6 Now add the cut-out pieces and pin everything in place.

The outside edges are now no longer in a square format. This erratic outline could become part of the new design or you could trim back the edges to a square or rectangular format.

It's surprising the variations you can achieve with a very simple shape like a diamond. Stitch the pieces together with hand and/or machine embroidery, neatening the edges to finish by turning them under.

EXTENSION EXERCISE

Work on a more complex shape – a flowerhead, perhaps?

For more information on machine stitching, see Further Reading, page 80.

EXPLORING FURTHER – YOUR PERSONAL WORK

Always be prepared to try different arrangements. Digital photographs can remind you of your original design if you want to return to it.

Working with different techniques can throw up new ideas and fresh avenues to explore. Also, when you attempt to combine contrasting processes, unexpected results occur.

Having discovered a technique that really appeals to you, focus on it, experiment and explore its possibilities. In this way you'll use it as an expressive tool for your creative ideas.

Above: The four layers of fabric have been moved off-centre with the cut-out sections placed on the top layer to change and enhance the design.

Right: The finished sample with the cut-out pieces applied and hand and machine threads echoing the diamond design.

CHAPTER 5

Challenging imagery

The challenge in this final chapter is how to achieve work that is surprising, dynamic and distinctive so that the viewer says 'Wow! What is all this about?'

To attain the 'surprise' that Jean Dubuffet talks of, we will explore ways of achieving unique and personal work by helping you express your responses to the world around you and bringing these into your art work.

But first we will analyse where your inspiration comes from. Your response to different experiences will probably fall into one of the following four categories.

THE REPRESENTATIONAL ARTIST

This means that your inspiration comes from external influences, the actual physical world around you that you interpret objectively: a landscape you have seen, an event you have experienced.

THE ABSTRACT ARTIST

Your art work is usually based on an idea or a concept. You may wish to explore the abstract concepts of colour, line, form and texture. Music can also stimulate an abstract response.

THE EMOTIONAL ARTIST

This work reflects the artist's interpretation of their surroundings in a very personal way as they react emotionally to events, people and feelings. The sense, for example, of dread or excitement can be vividly expressed through the work.

THE MATERIAL ARTIST

The pure joy of exploring the possibilities of your chosen medium is expressed in this category – no external influences, no emotional responses. Does your work fit neatly into one of these definitions, or do you straddle some of them? It's helpful to identify your main source of inspiration because it enables you to become more objective and self-critical about your working practice. Being aware of the other categories will give you a broader vision and appreciation of other artists' work. For many of us our art work reflects a combination of two categories.

We'll now return to the main theme of this chapter, challenging imagery, and will start with a simple fun exercise to get the grey matter working and create some contrasting images. The results of this lateral thinking exercise will have some unexpected outcomes – and we're looking for 'surprises'.

'What I expect from any work of art is that it surprises me...'

Jean Dubuffet

'Still Life 'L'. 60 x 48 cm (24 x 19 in).
The letters of the words STILL LIFE contrast with the objects (apples, bowls and candlesticks). Can you spot the letters? If not, go to Jae's page on www.d4daisy.com and we'll show you.

SKILL DEVELOPMENT 1

Word play

AIM

To create a paper collage using two random and contrasting words that spring out from the word association exercise.

MATERIALS

- Pad
- Pencil
- Collection of magazines
- Scissors
- Paper glue
- Sheet of paper, A4 (Letter) size
- Drawing and painting media (optional).

LIST

1. book
2. print (circled)
3. newspaper
4. crossword
5. grid
6. scaffolding
7. building
8. home
9. number 5
10. street (circled)

METHOD

You will need a partner for this exercise.

1 Start by choosing a word. It can be something that you see – the more strange the word, the more fun the exercise becomes. Write this word at the top of your pad.

2 Your partner responds spontaneously with the first word that comes to mind. You write this word below the first word on your list.

3 Now it's your turn to respond with another spontaneous word and add it to your list. Your partner then answers, and so on.

4 Make a list of ten words. If your partner also wants to make a collage, you both repeat the process and he or she makes their own list.

5 With your list in front of you, ring your second word and your last word. These will be the starting points for your paper collage. The words will be unrelated and it can be an enormous challenge to combine them.

6 The magazines now come into use as you find appropriate images to fit the contrasting words. Arrange them on the sheet of paper. Be imaginative as to how you interpret the two words. There are no rules.

7 When you have a harmonious design, glue the images in place.

You can add paint and sketches to pull the collage together.

This fun exercise frees the mind and will help you become more flexible when thinking about your subject matter. However, even more useful is the following activity, which is an absolute must!

One interpretation of the ringed words on the list – 'Print' and 'Street'. Newspaper images of street scenes form the basis of this idea. They were strengthened by backing them with card. They will then stand upright to create a 'street' from the printed street images.

EXTENSION EXERCISE

A mind map

(With acknowledgement to Tony Buzan – see Further Reading, page 80)

When you are starting a new piece of work, you will have the germ of an idea. To encourage flexibility and expansion of that idea, a mind map is a great way to start.

Your theme needs to take the form of one word. In this illustration, 'Beach' has been selected. This word could represent a bunch of holiday snaps or sketches of a memorable day out. It is placed in the centre of a large piece of plain paper (A3, double Letter-size), with a ring around it.

You now begin to think of all your associations with 'Beach'. Let your mind run free. These thoughts are attached by small links springing from the main circle. Aim for ten words.

Now pursue each of these words and attach more thoughts until you have a page of ideas on 'Beach'. Several words may repeat themselves at the outer limits of the mind map and these could be the foundation for your design. Your original central word will have been expanded in unexpected ways, giving you a host of new ideas to explore.

A piece of work and an idea may move a long way from your original thought but that's what innovation and individuality is all about.

EXPLORING FURTHER
– YOUR PERSONAL WORK

The mind map is a useful device if you have a creative block. It can be used to expand ideas around a technique you are working with and which you want to move forward. It can also help solve a problem during the development of a piece of work. By highlighting the problem in the centre of the map, options can be identified and a resolution can often be the result.

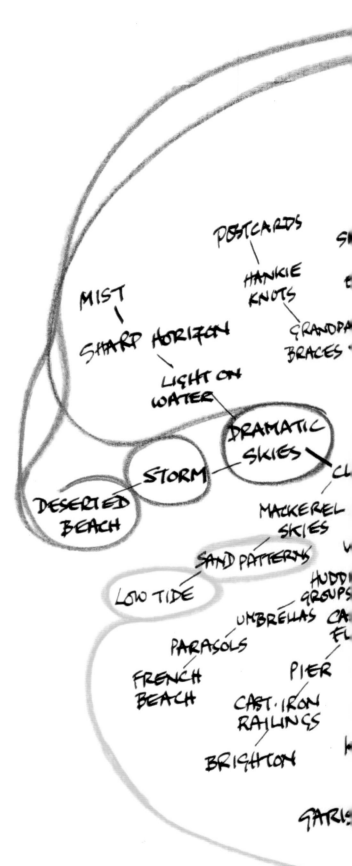

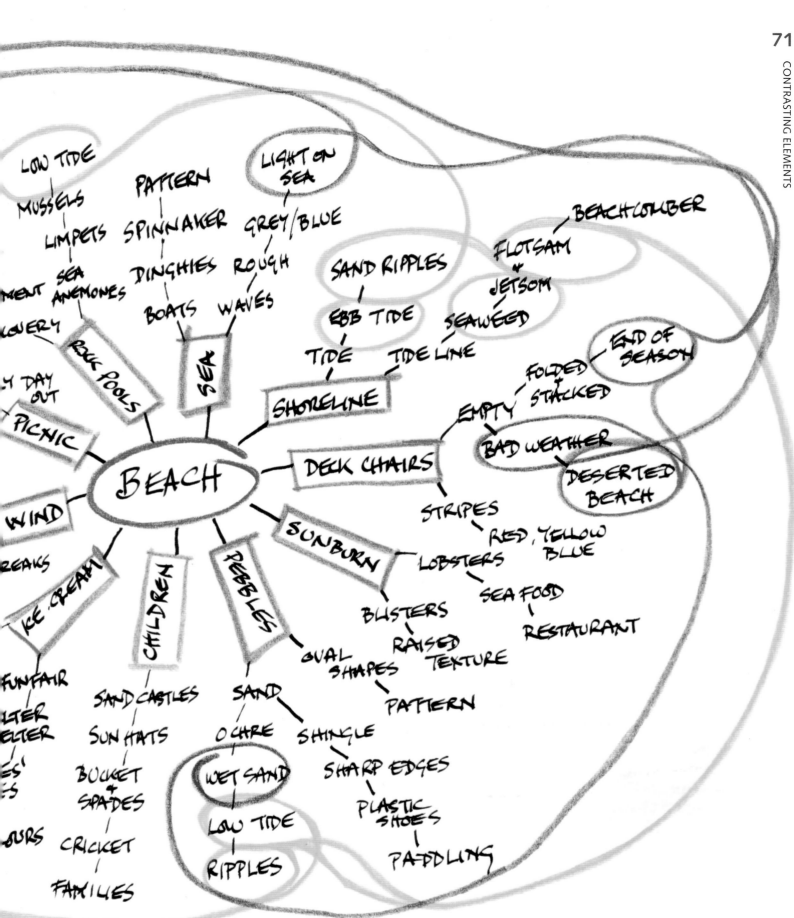

A Mind Map exploring the theme 'Beach'
offers diverse avenues to explore.

SKILL DEVELOPMENT 2

Creating a memory box

We're now going to get personal and concentrate on you, your life and how to bring into your art work the contrasts that you experience every day.

AIM

To continue the idea of contrasting imagery by gathering together a collection of diverse objects over a period of seven days, in order to create a memory box.

MATERIALS

- A box lid, minimum A4 (Letter) size

- A collection of items reflecting everyday activities

- PVA glue

- Acrylic or watercolour paint and brush.

Top: A random selection of items collected during the week including threads, leaves, wood, string, bottle, puzzle pieces.

Above: Items arranged, painted and stuck in place. Cheerful colours suggest a 'good' week.

METHOD

1   Each day, collect items that reflect your day. It could be something you saw or experienced. It might be your personal reaction to something you have read or heard. Place them at random in the box lid.

2   After the seven days, begin to arrange the objects in the box lid. You will probably discard some things, keeping only those that made a real impact on you. You may want to paint or line the box lid with colour to emphasise how you felt about your week. The objects could also be painted to emphasise your reaction to them.

3   When the arrangement looks good, stick everything firmly in place.

4   If the collection lacks continuity, think about painting everything one colour. Perhaps it rained all week – grey may be appropriate!

This memory box will reflect a small period of your personal life on an intimate scale.

'Drawing is like making an expressive gesture with the advantage of permanence.'

Henri Matisse

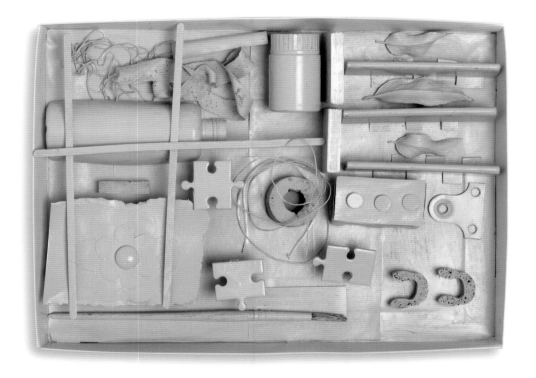

Above: It rained all week!

EXTENSION EXERCISE

You could try making other memory boxes to cover special events like holidays or family gatherings.

EXPLORING FURTHER – YOUR PERSONAL WORK

This leads straight into the very last activity in the book, and possibly the most important, depending on how passionate you are to move your work forward and make it more personal and meaningful.

SKILL DEVELOPMENT 3

Sketchbooks

We have almost come full circle because, in the first paragraph of the book, 'contrasts' that occur in your everyday life are mentioned. The question is: How to capture these contrasting events and feelings and use them as inspiration for your new work?

Sketchbooks – those intimate, creative, private journals – are the answer. They are a personal record of your responses to events, people, feelings and actions.

AIM

To notate the contrasts in your daily life through sketches over a period of a week.

MATERIALS

- Sketchbook

- Mark-making materials: charcoal, pencils, pens, biros, felt-tips, crayons, inks etc.

METHOD

Keep your sketchbook uncluttered. Just use marks, symbols and drawings – no extra images such as photographs or postcards; they are too impersonal. Your own marks and scratches, blobs and splashes are the best way to make sense of the world around you. Studio or office detritus, perhaps part of a train ticket or a shop receipt, can be added; it might be key to the day's events.

If you are intimidated by the blank white page, paint a pale wash all over it to start. This will help those first tentative marks. Another method is to stick on some strips of paper before drawing, or even to tear up the page and re-piece it.

Most important of all is to make the commitment and start your sketchbook.

At some time during the day, think back to the main event that had an impact upon you. It could be a visual stimulus, a colour, an event or something that you made you angry or sad.

Positive reactions demand a positive mark or scribble whereas negative happenings or emotions will demand contrasting drawings.

These marks will reflect the Matisse quotation – they are gestures like hand and arm movements. They need not be illustrative and can be non-figurative to reflect your mood. Cross and annoyed could be an agitated mark but, if the mood was calm, a smooth comfortable curve in a peaceful colour would be more appropriate.

Make sure your marks fill the page and even run off the edge of the page if necessary.

Don't be afraid to overlap the drawn marks. What seemed important at the beginning of the day may fade into insignificance later and you may wish to draw over it. So don't erase anything.

Two pages from one of my sketchbooks. The open sketchbook shows two consecutive days in my life.

Top image: A drawing in charcoal of part of some gym equipment – my regular 7am. visit. Red paint – working on a small textile. Blue square – sunny day. Some black anxious marks in Indian ink – things not going so well on a personal level.

Bottom image: Next day – bad news – strong black ink marks are trapping other more optimistic feelings.

As a guideline, let's try an example of a random day.

Every day, aim to sketch, paint, scribble and/or make marks that represent four contrasting responses: an action, a mood or feeling, a visual stimulus and an event. It will continually surprise you how different each day can be. If you can't get to your sketchbook at the end of a day, try to catch up the following day. If you always carry some paper and a pencil with you, you can make some jottings during the day and staple them into the sketchbook later.

As this is your personal visual diary, there are no rules. You may find it a challenge to start but with practice it will become easier.

Will there be material there for you to work from?

Perhaps not immediately but by persevering and concentrating on your reactions to your world and attempting to translate them into a visual form, your awareness of your personal feelings will become more apparent and will, in the long run, add depth and a strong individual signature to your art work.

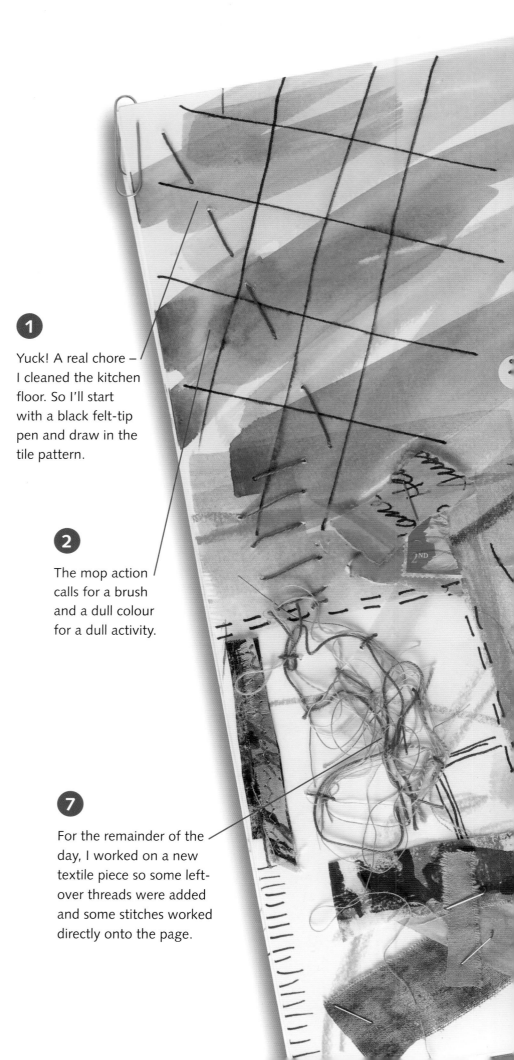

1 Yuck! A real chore – I cleaned the kitchen floor. So I'll start with a black felt-tip pen and draw in the tile pattern.

2 The mop action calls for a brush and a dull colour for a dull activity.

7 For the remainder of the day, I worked on a new textile piece so some left-over threads were added and some stitches worked directly onto the page.

3

The post arrived and one of my pieces of work has been selected for an exhibition – hurray! One cheerful orange mark rising through the page.

4

I then met a friend for coffee. We chatted, so a circle isolates the two of us (intimate) with to and fro conversation.

5

On the way home the sun came out and the patterns of the sunlight through the leaves was beautiful.

6

But, when I arrived back, I was furious because the cat had walked across the clean kitchen floor with muddy paws.

EXPLORING FURTHER – YOUR PERSONAL WORK

The daily commitment of keeping a sketchbook means that your art work is a priority in your life. By giving it this focus of attention, your work cannot fail to have added depth and meaning. Not only will you gain confidence in mark-making but you will think more profoundly about your life. Your work can then become the vehicle through which you will begin to express yourself in a much more personal and individual way. As you look back through the sketchbook, it will be like looking through a window at your thoughts, feelings and actions which will, in time, become a valuable resource for your art work.

The onward journey

My aim is to give you, by working through this book, the confidence to develop innovative, exciting work. As you experiment with unusual juxtapositions of colour, design elements, materials, techniques and imagery you will begin to explore new avenues which will help you break away from the conventional. When you discover an approach that really engages you, explore it more fully. In this way you will begin to find a distinctive and individual way of expressing yourself. Through the use of contrasting elements in your art work, you can engage with, and express through your work, the contrasts that you experience in everyday life.

Good luck!

'Art washes away the dust of everyday life.'

Pablo Picasso

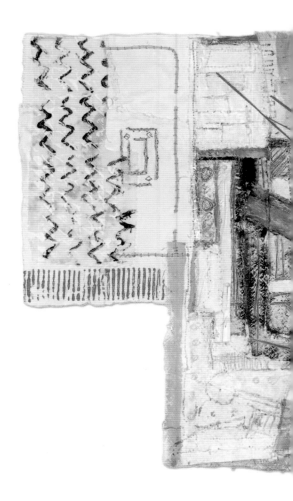

'Site Development Series II and III'. 65 x 120 cm (25 x 47 in). The materials and the method are the same as those for the other Site Development pieces on Page 51.

The series follows the building of a new house from the planning stage, through the ground-works, to the interior development.

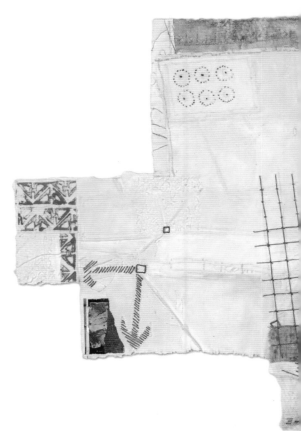